W9-CSR-166

TRUE STORIES OF
Animal Oddities

BY ARNOLD RINGSTAD

Published by The Child's World®
1980 Lookout Drive • Mankato, MN 56003-1705
800-599-READ • www.childsworld.com

Acknowledgments
The Child's World®: Mary Berendes, Publishing Director
Red Line Editorial: Editorial direction
The Design Lab: Design
Amnet: Production

Photographs ©: Stuart Clarke/Rex Features/AP Images, cover
(bottom), 1 (bottom), 5; Amy Bauernseind/New England
Aquarium/AP Images, back cover (bottom), 3 (bottom right),
10; San Antonio Zoo/AP Images, cover (top), 1 (top), 13; Peter
Gordon/Rex Features/AP Images, back cover (top), 2–3, 15;
Hai Qunying/ICHPL Imaginechina/AP Images, cover (center), 19;
PhotoDisc, back cover (top), 3 (top right), 14, 18, 23; Chris Perry/
NASA/AP Images, 4, 21; Thinkstock, 6; CB2/ZOB/WENN.
com/Newscom, 7; Kevin Scott Ramos/Guinness World Records/
AP Images, 8; DigitalStock, 9; FoodIcons, 11; Guinness World
Records/AP Images, 17

ISBN 9781626873599
LCCN 2014930698

Printed in the United States of America
Mankato, MN
July, 2014
PA02225

ABOUT THE AUTHOR

*Arnold Ringstad lives in
Minnesota. His cat behaves
oddly sometimes.*

CONTENTS

ANIMAL ODDITIES

*Some animals are **bizarre**. It can be fun to learn about unusual creatures. Orange sheep, hippos with pink boots, and space frogs are just a few examples. Read on to learn more about these and other stories of animal **oddities**.*

A space frog
one animal od

Orange Sheep

If you have been out in the country, you may have seen a flock of sheep. Their white, gray, or black wool makes them easy to spot. Farmer John Heard's sheep are like any others. But they are different in one big way. Their wool is bright orange!

Heard lives near Devon, a city in England. He owns several hundred sheep. Over time, he began to notice that some were missing. In just a few years, thieves had stolen 200. The sheep are worth nearly $230 each. The thefts had cost Heard a lot of money. He knew he had to find a way to stop people from stealing them.

He finally figured out a smart way to save his sheep. Heard knew thieves stole sheep to sell them. But if he painted the sheep a weird color, everyone would know the sheep belonged to him. Sheep buyers would know the animals were stolen.

The orange dye he used does not harm the sheep. And after he started using it, not a single sheep was stolen!

These orange sheep are unusual creatures.

The Capybara Pet

Many people keep guinea pigs as pets. But not as many people know about capybaras. If you have not seen one, you might think you are looking at a giant guinea pig!

Capybaras live in South America. You can find them near water. Capybaras also live in zoos across the world. But few capybaras are kept as pets. One person who does keep one is Melanie Typaldos of Buda, Texas. Her pet is named Caplin Rous. He may be the most famous capybara on the planet!

Typaldos walks Caplin on a leash. He can even do tricks! Typaldos writes a **blog** about her life with Caplin. The animal also stars in videos on the Internet. Caplin helps teach people about capybaras.

Capybaras are unusual pets.

Caplin takes a treat from his owner, Melanie Typaldos.

The World's Tallest Dog

Dogs come in many sizes. Some are tiny Chihuahuas. Others are giant Great Danes. These big dogs stand about 30 inches (76 cm) tall. Large dogs are not usually odd. But one Great Dane from Michigan is truly amazing. His name is Zeus.

Zeus is so tall he can reach the kitchen faucet!

Zeus's owner has to fill up his food bowl often.

Zeus belongs to Denise Doorlag of Otsego, Michigan. He is 44 inches (112 cm) tall at his shoulder. That's nearly as tall as a six-year-old boy. On his back legs, Zeus stands 7 feet 4 inches (2.2 meters). That is taller than most professional basketball players! He has an appetite to match his size. Zeus eats 12 cups of food a day!

Doorlag says some people think Zeus is too big to be a dog: "It's fun to see people's reactions . . . they think that he really is a horse!"

A Halloween Lobster

Catching lobsters is big business in New England. In 2012, people caught 123 million pounds (56 million kg) of them in Maine alone. Almost all lobsters are green. Lobsters with unusual colors are rare. Scientists estimate only one lobster in 2 million is blue. They believe one lobster in 30 million is yellow. But in 2012, lobsterman Dana Duhaime caught an even rarer one off the coast of Massachusetts.

Duhaime found a lobster that was half orange and half black. Only one lobster in 50 to 100 million has these colors.

This lobster's combination of colors is very rare.

Because of its coloring, some called it a Halloween lobster. Duhaime nicknamed her "Pinchy."

Duhaime showed the lobster to a **biologist**. The biologist brought it to the New England Aquarium. The aquarium revealed the lobster to the public on Halloween in 2012.

WHY NOT RED?
Many people think lobsters are red. However, they only turn this color when they are cooked. The heat changes the chemicals that form the lobster's shell. The chemical change brings out the red color.

Lobsters only turn red when they're cooked.

The Two-Headed Turtle

You have probably seen twin humans before. But did you know animals can have twins, too? In 2013, a mother turtle at the San Antonio Zoo in Texas laid her eggs. Until the eggs hatched, no one knew she had a pair of twins in one egg. But her twins did not completely separate. Instead, one of her babies had two heads!

The tiny turtle was just a little bigger than a quarter. Zoo workers said that the turtle could eat and swim just fine. They did not expect any health problems. They also said the two heads got along well.

The turtle has been very popular among zoo guests. The zoo even set up a Facebook page for it!

This turtle's two heads get along well,
zookeepers say.

A Hippo with Pink Boots

Some hippos call Tanzania home.

The African country of Tanzania is full of amazing animals. Elephants, zebras, lions, and chimpanzees are just a few animals that live there. Tanzania has many national parks where people can easily view these creatures. One of the most amazing animals is the hippopotamus, or hippo. These huge mammals are great swimmers. In fact, their name means "river horse." They are quick on land, too.

Hippos are usually a grey color. However, you may find one odd hippo at one of Tanzania's **game reserves**. It looks like it is wearing pink boots!

This is what a photographer saw in 2011. A group of hippos was standing near a river. One hippo in the group had pink legs and feet. It is not rare for hippos to have some pink spots on their bodies. Sometimes a disease can change a hippo's skin color. But usually the spots are random. In this case, the spots covered all four legs and feet. The photographer was able to take several pictures before the hippos left.

HASTY HIPPOS
Hippos have large bodies and short legs. They look like they would run slowly. However, they can actually run as fast as people!

This hippo looks like it has pink boots on.

The World's Smallest Dog

Dogs can be very large. Zeus from Michigan is the world's largest dog. But what about the other end of the size range? In September 2013, Guinness World Records named the world's smallest dog. She is a Chihuahua named Milly. She lives with her owner in Puerto Rico. Just how small is she? Milly is only 3.8 inches (9.65 cm) tall. In other words, it would take more than 11 Millys to equal the height of one Zeus!

Milly's owner is Vanesa Semler. Her dog weighs just 1 pound (0.5 kg). Milly was born in December 2011. At first, Semler says, Milly was much smaller. She weighed less than 1 ounce (28 grams). The puppy could fit into a teaspoon!

Milly may be small, but Semler said she still surprises people. She said, "People are amazed when they see her because she is so small, and she has a big personality." Milly sleeps in a baby crib. The dog loves to pose for photos. She sometimes even sticks her tongue out when people take her picture!

Milly is barely as tall as a sneaker!

A Lion or a Dog?

Zoos are great places to find animals you cannot normally see. They are often the only place to see a lion, elephant, or tiger. However, what if the animal in the lion's pen is not a lion? Visitors to a zoo in central China asked this question in 2013.

People who looked inside the cage labeled "African Lion" saw a large, hairy animal. They were shocked when the animal made a noise. It was a bark!

The zoo was trying to use a big dog as a lion. The dog was a Tibetan mastiff. This breed of dog is very large and hairy. Visitors were upset about the switch. One said, "The zoo is absolutely trying to cheat us. They are trying to disguise dogs as lions."

ZOO MIX-UP
The dog was not the only mixed-up animal at the zoo. Another dog was in the wolf cage. A white fox was taking the place of a leopard.

Lions are common zoo animals.

That's not a lion! It's a dog!

Space Frog

In September 2013, scientists in the United States prepared to send a robotic **probe** into space. They got ready to launch a Minotaur V rocket. This 81-foot (24.6 m) rocket would carry the probe to the moon. Scientists at the **launchpad** in Virginia were excited to learn more about the moon. However, they did not expect an **amphibian** visitor at the launch.

Even though the launch was at night, the rocket was so bright it lit up the area. Photos of the liftoff showed a frog flying through the air near the rocket. It may have been blown into the air by the amazing power of the launch.

It was not surprising that a frog was nearby. The launchpad dumps water under the rocket at launch. This helps to soften the noise from the launch. Otherwise, the power of the sound could damage the launchpad. The frog may have been living in the water next to the launch pad.

BEWARE OF THE ROCKET!

There have been other stories of animals near rocket launches. In 2009, a bat was seen holding onto a space shuttle. In 2013, a rocket test frightened a herd of cows.

A frog goes flying at a rocket launch.

amphibian (am-FIB-ee-un) An amphibian is an animal that lives both on land and in the water. A frog is one type of amphibian.

biologist (bi-AWL-oh-jist) A biologist is a scientist who studies living things. A biologist brought the Halloween lobster to the New England Aquarium.

bizarre (bih-ZAHR) Something that is bizarre is very strange. Some animals are quite bizarre.

blog (blawg) A blog is a personal Web site where people can write about whatever they wish. Caplin's owner writes a blog about living with a capybara.

game reserves (gaym ree-ZERVZ) Game reserves are areas set aside for watching and hunting animals. Hippos live on game reserves in Tanzania.

launchpad (LAWNCH-pad) A launchpad is the place where a rocket blasts off. Animals may live near a launchpad.

oddities (AW-di-teez) Oddities are strange things. Some animal stories are filled with oddities.

probe (prohb) A probe is a robot that collects information about space. A probe may travel to space on a rocket.

BOOKS

125 True Stories of Amazing Animals: Inspiring Tales of Animal Friendship and Four-Legged Heroes, Plus Crazy Animal Antics. Washington, DC: National Geographic, 2012.

125 True Stories of Amazing Pets: Inspiring Tales of Animal Friendship and Four-Legged Heroes, Plus Crazy Animal Antics. Washington, DC: National Geographic, 2014.

Newman, Aline Alexander. *Ape Escapes! and More True Stories of Animals Behaving Badly.* Washington, DC: National Geographic, 2012.

WEB SITES

Visit our Web site for links about animal oddities:
childsworld.com/links

Note to Parents, Teachers, and Librarians:
We routinely verify our Web links to make sure they are safe and active sites. So encourage your readers to check them out!